In Dedication to
Jacqueline "Jackie" Loi Lynton

*Gone but will never be forgotten,
you were loved so much.*

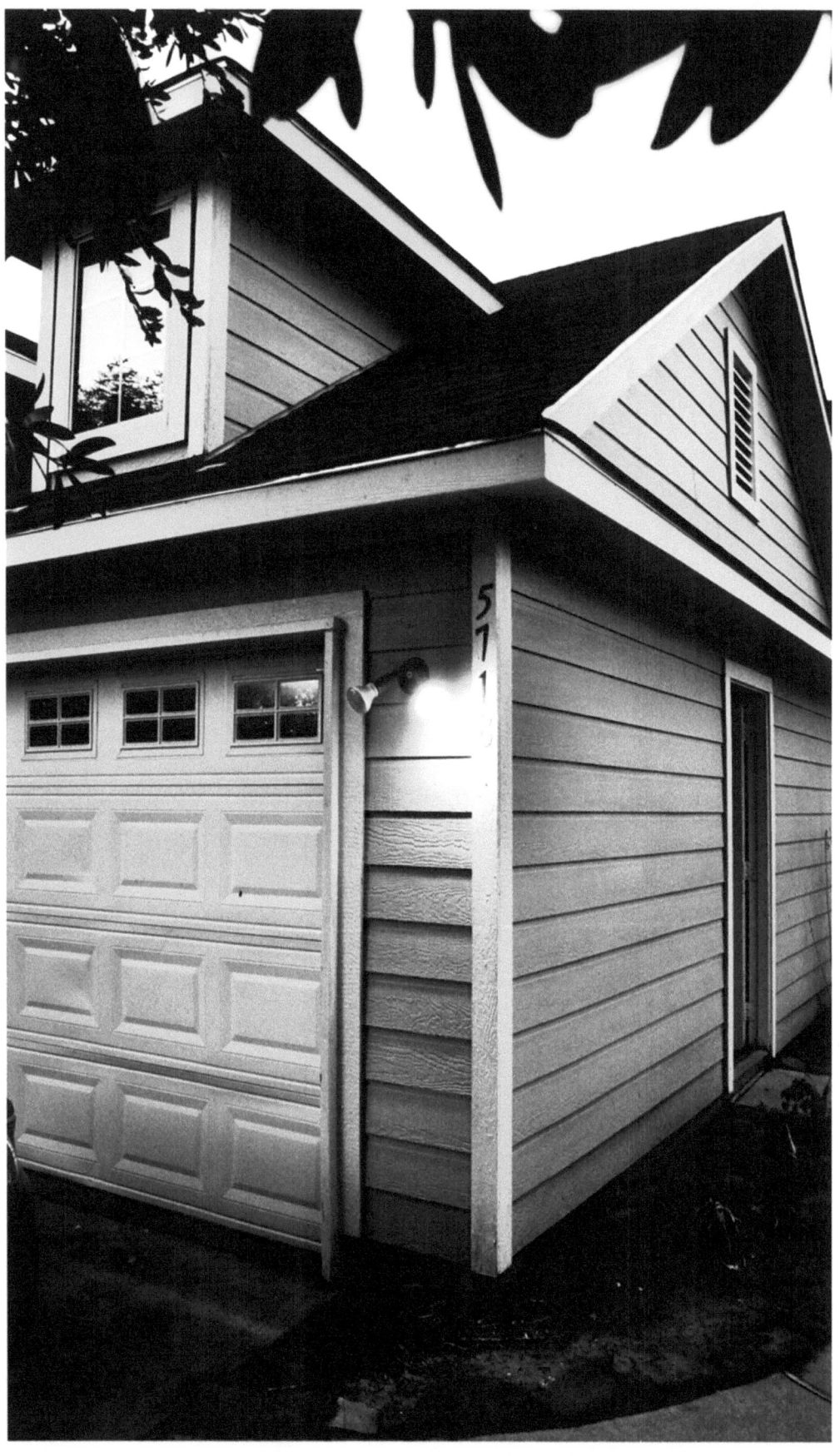

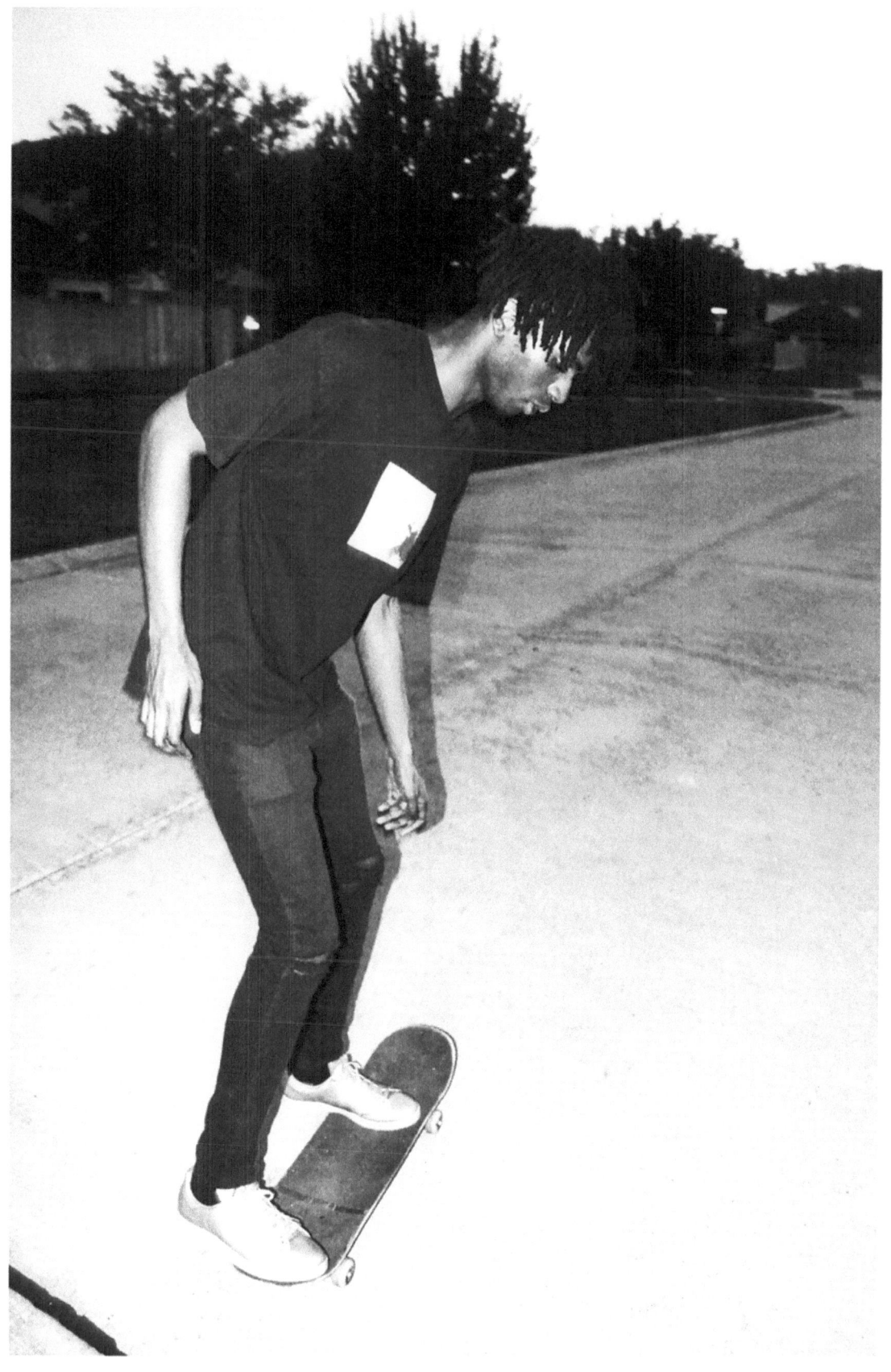

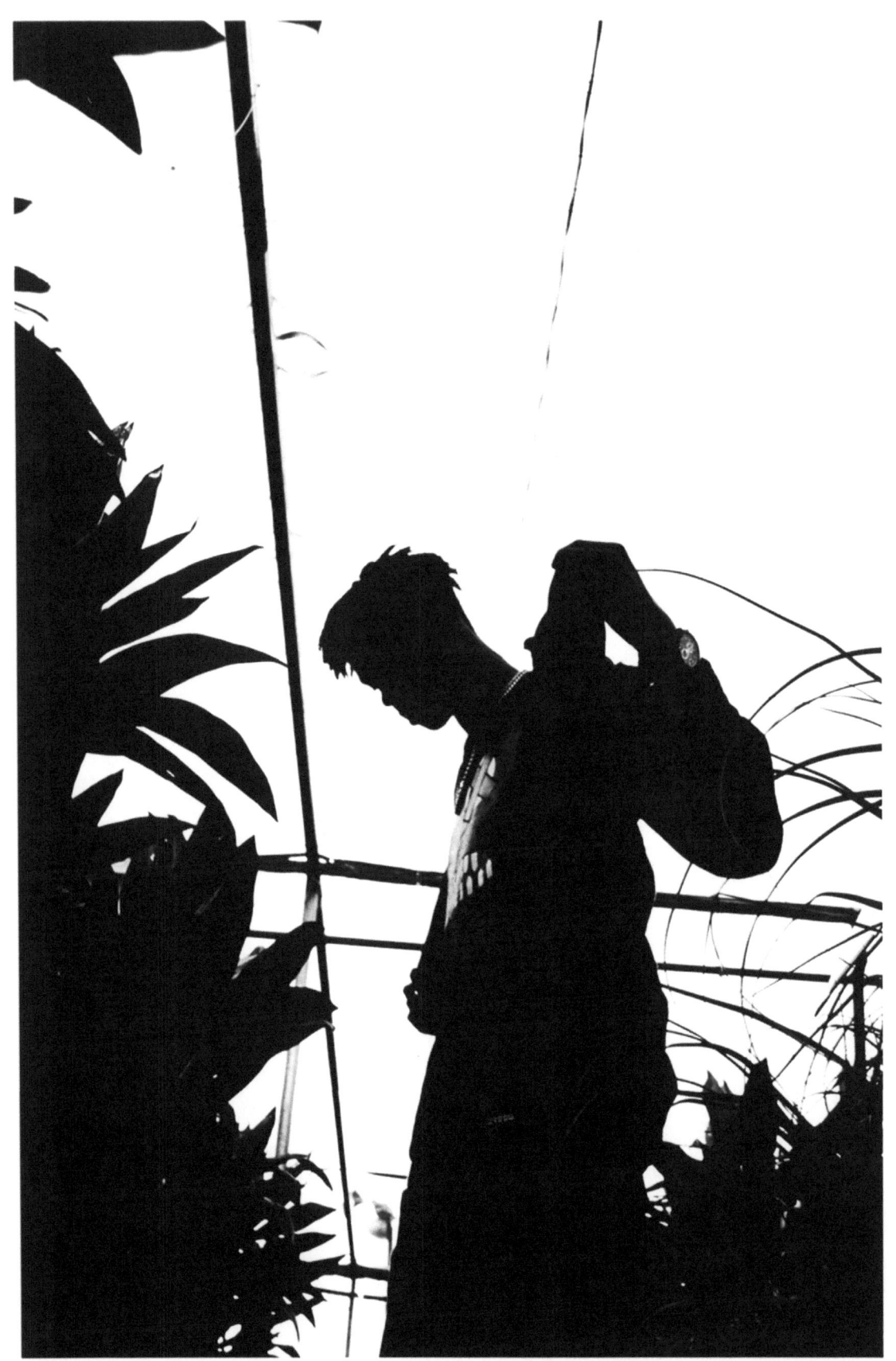

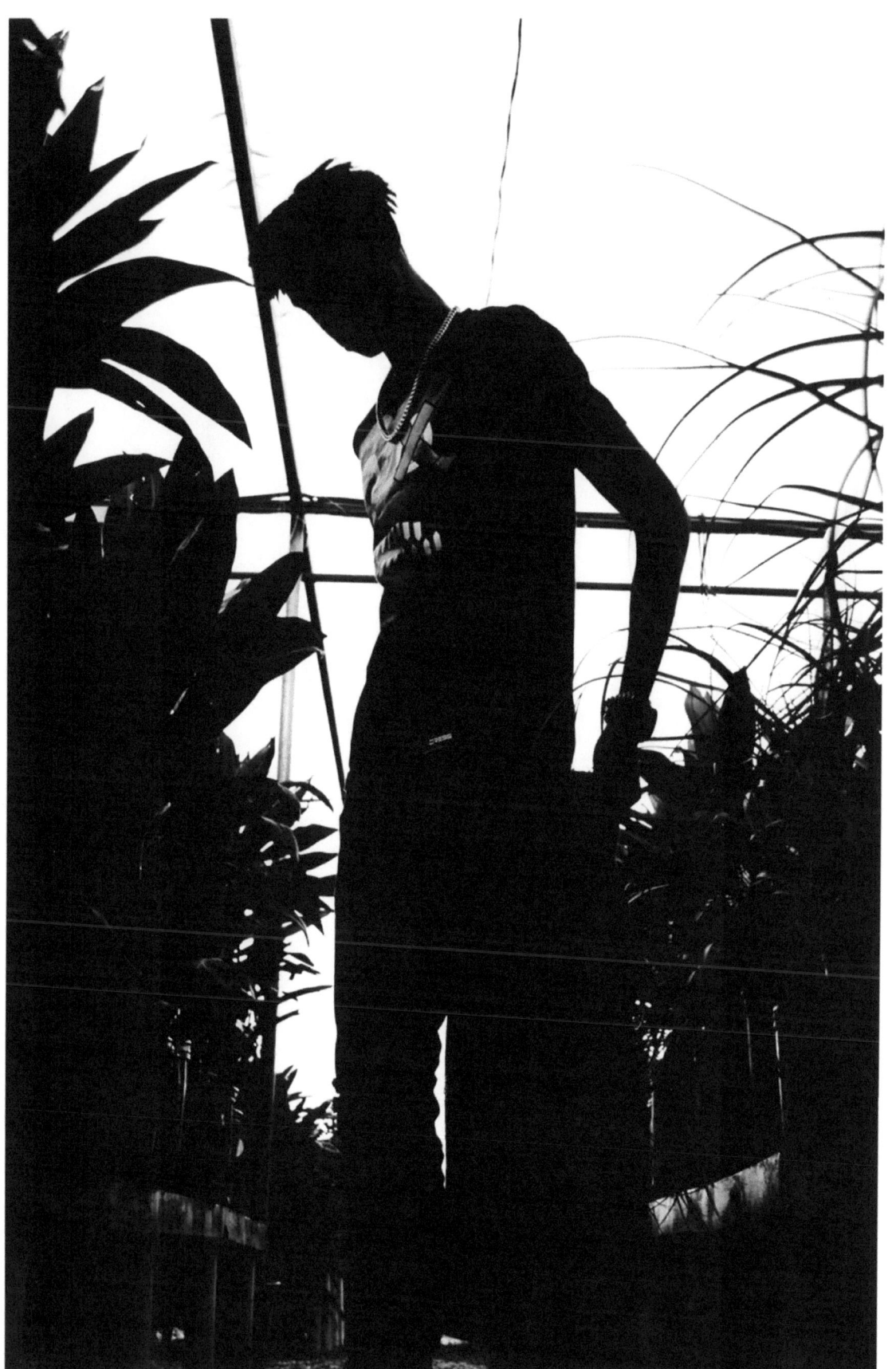

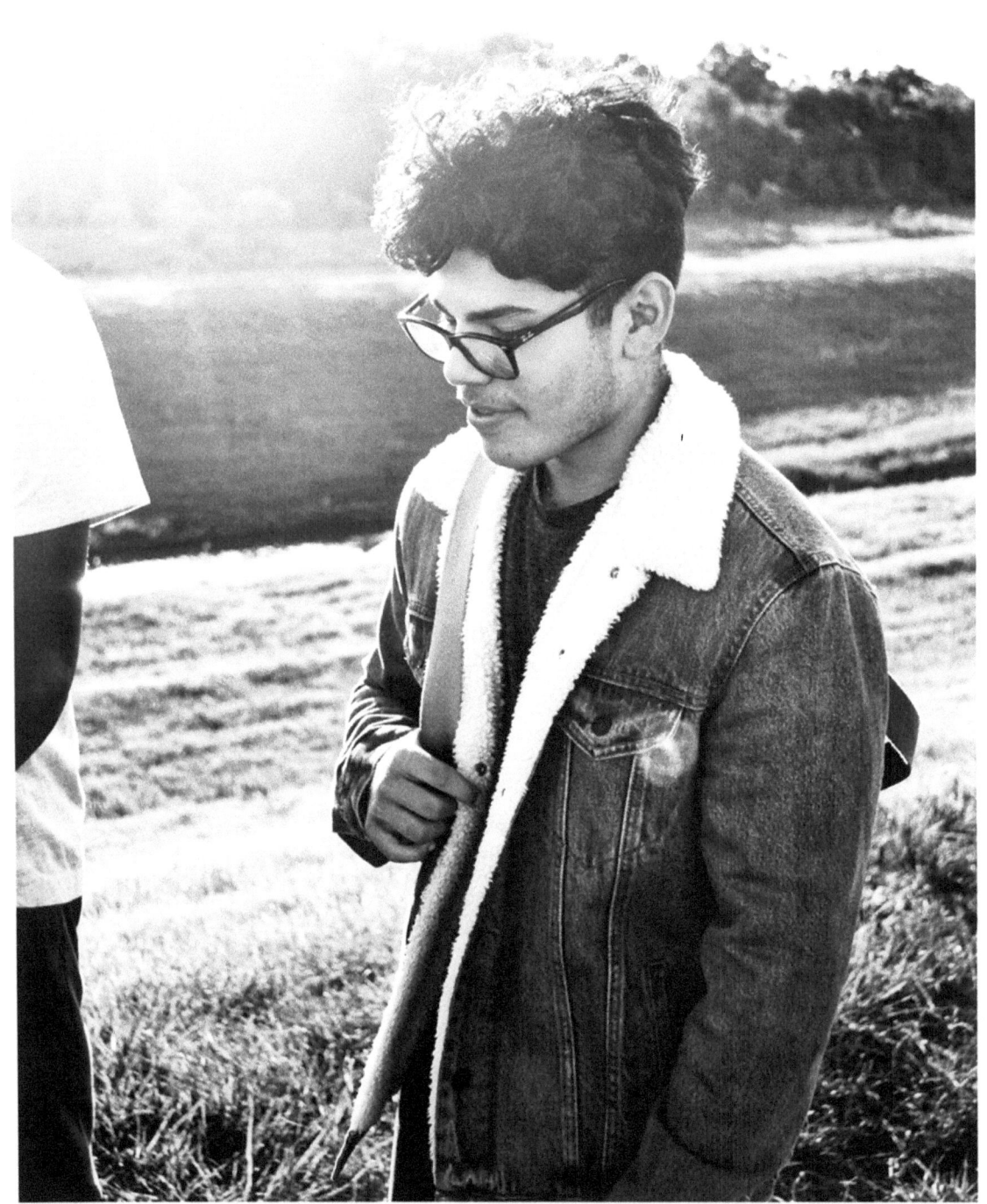

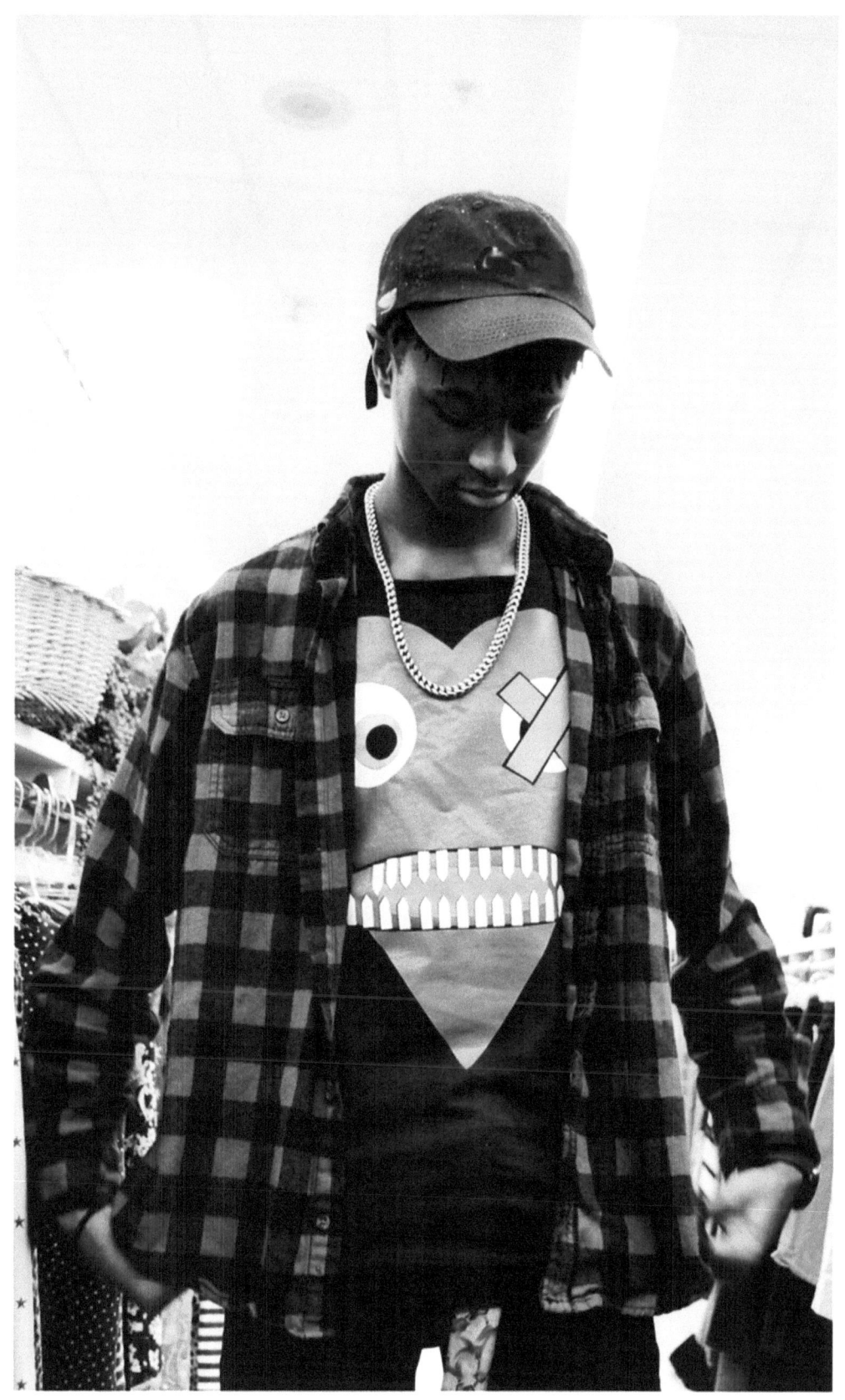

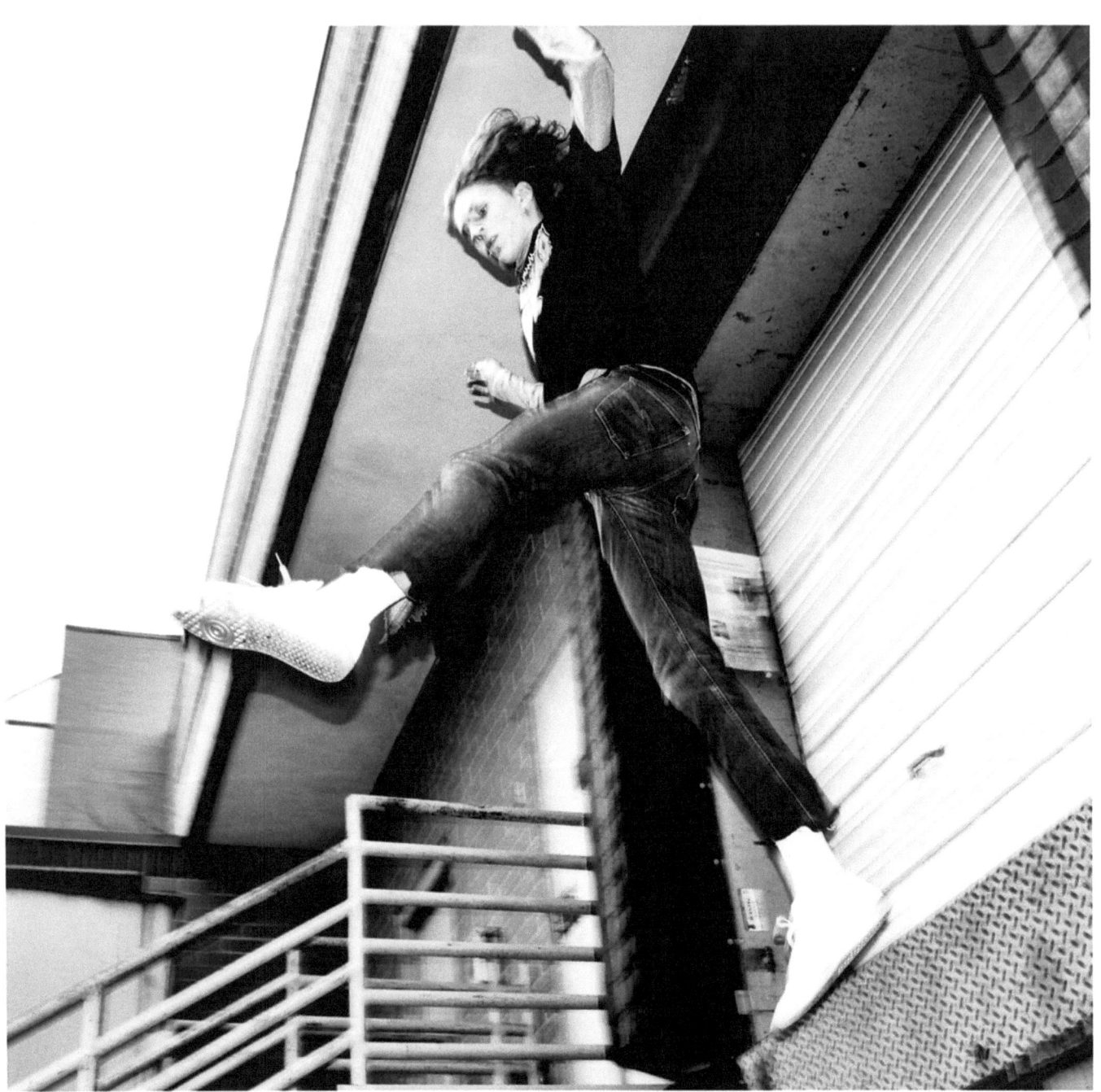

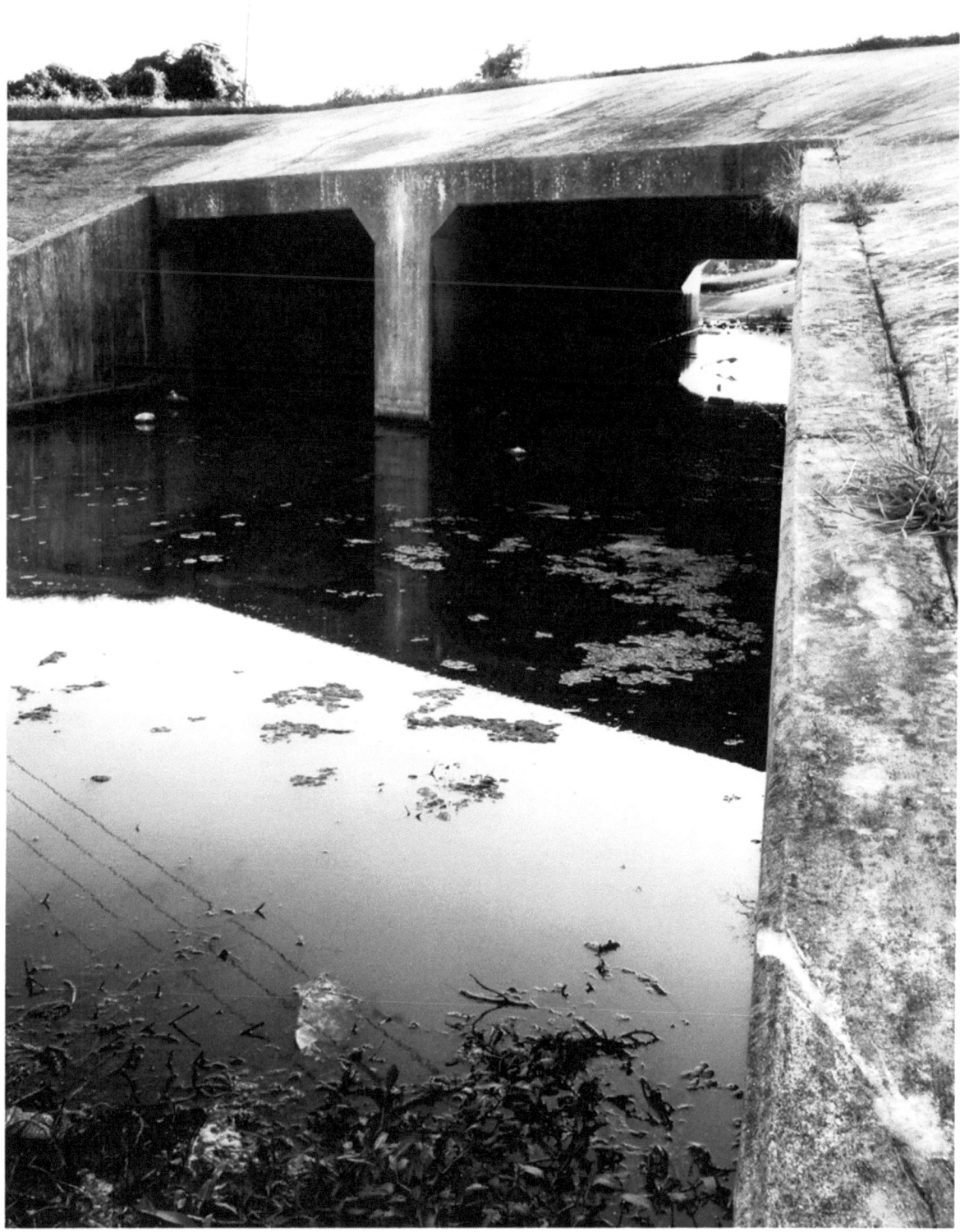

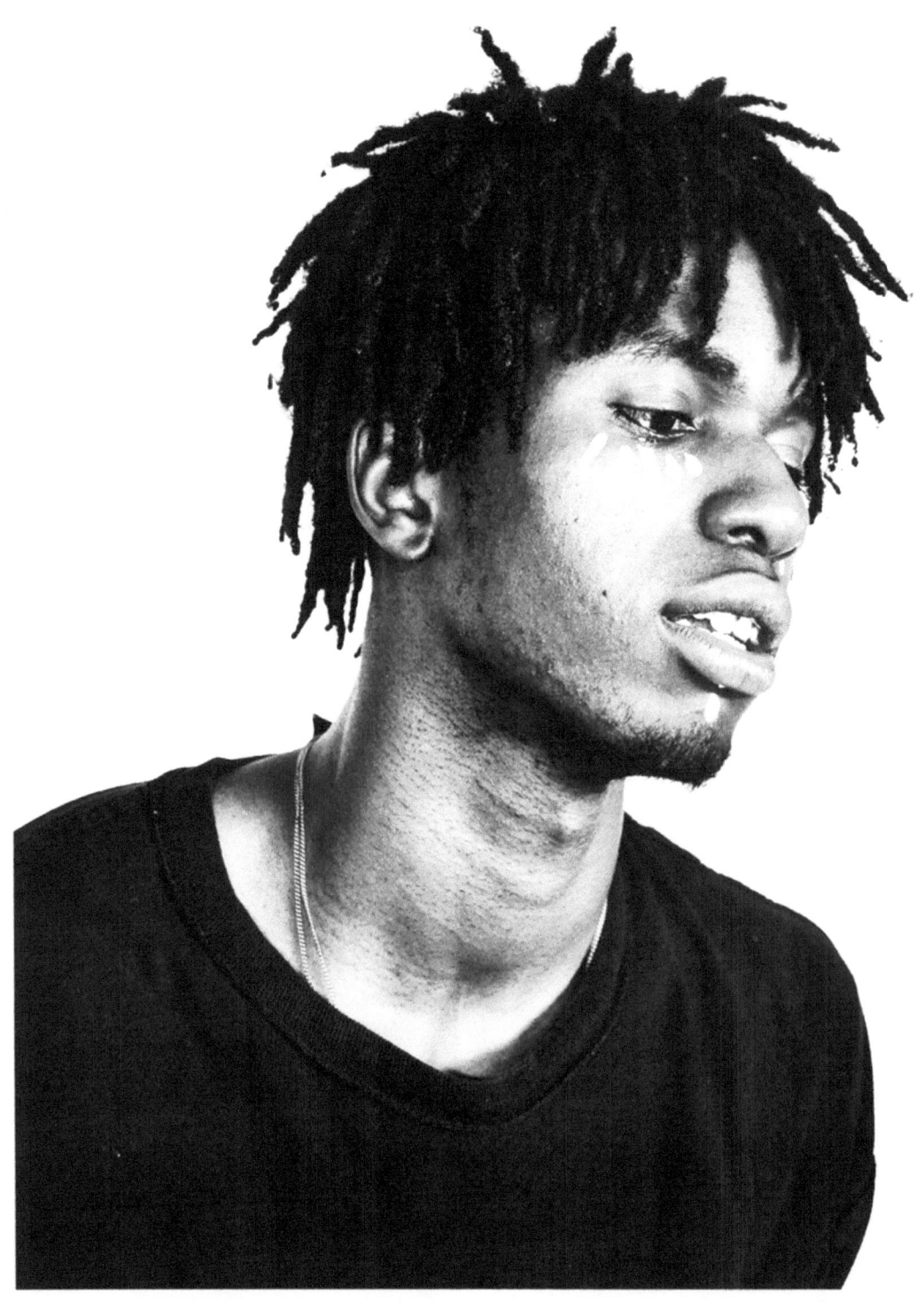

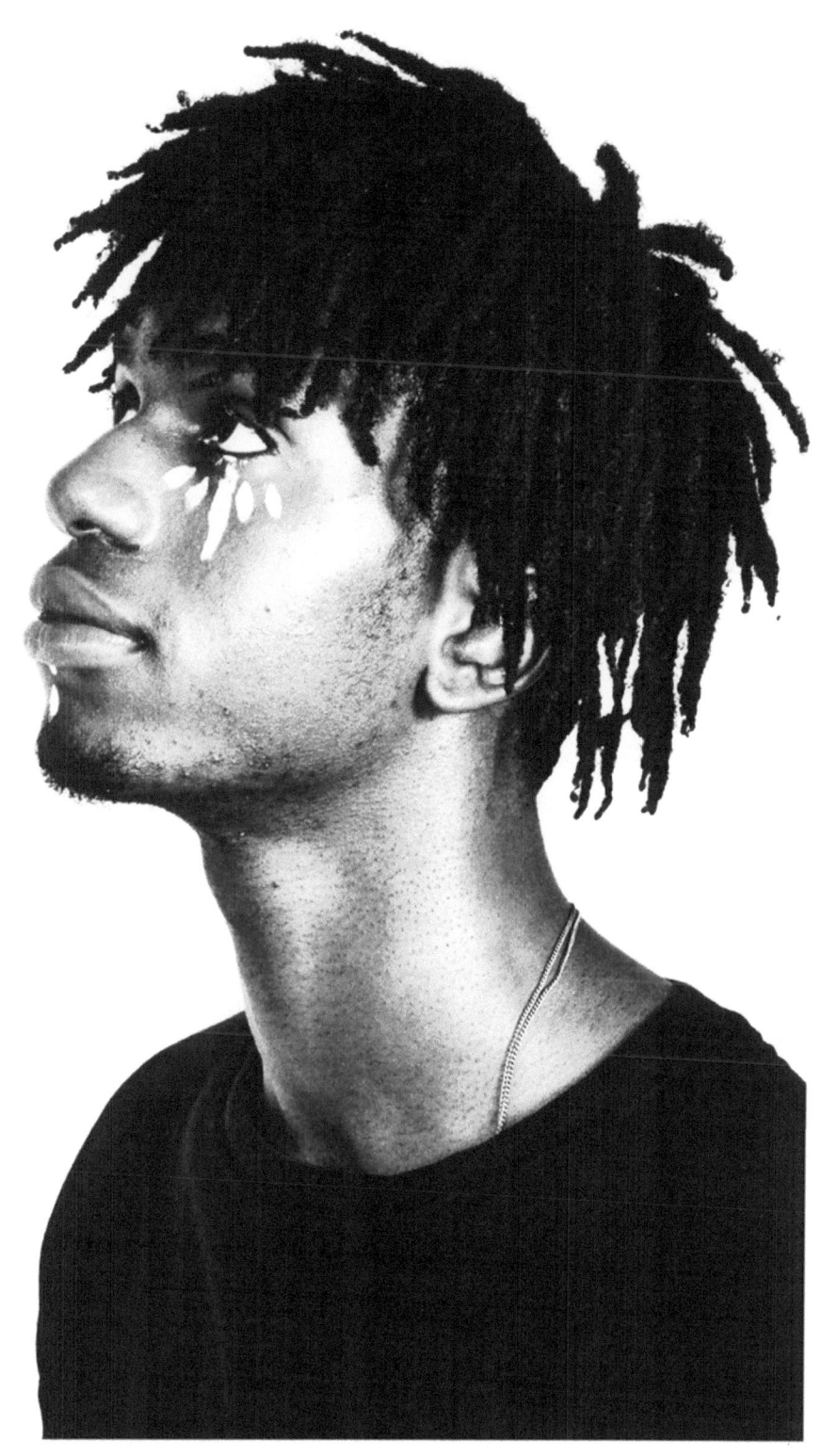

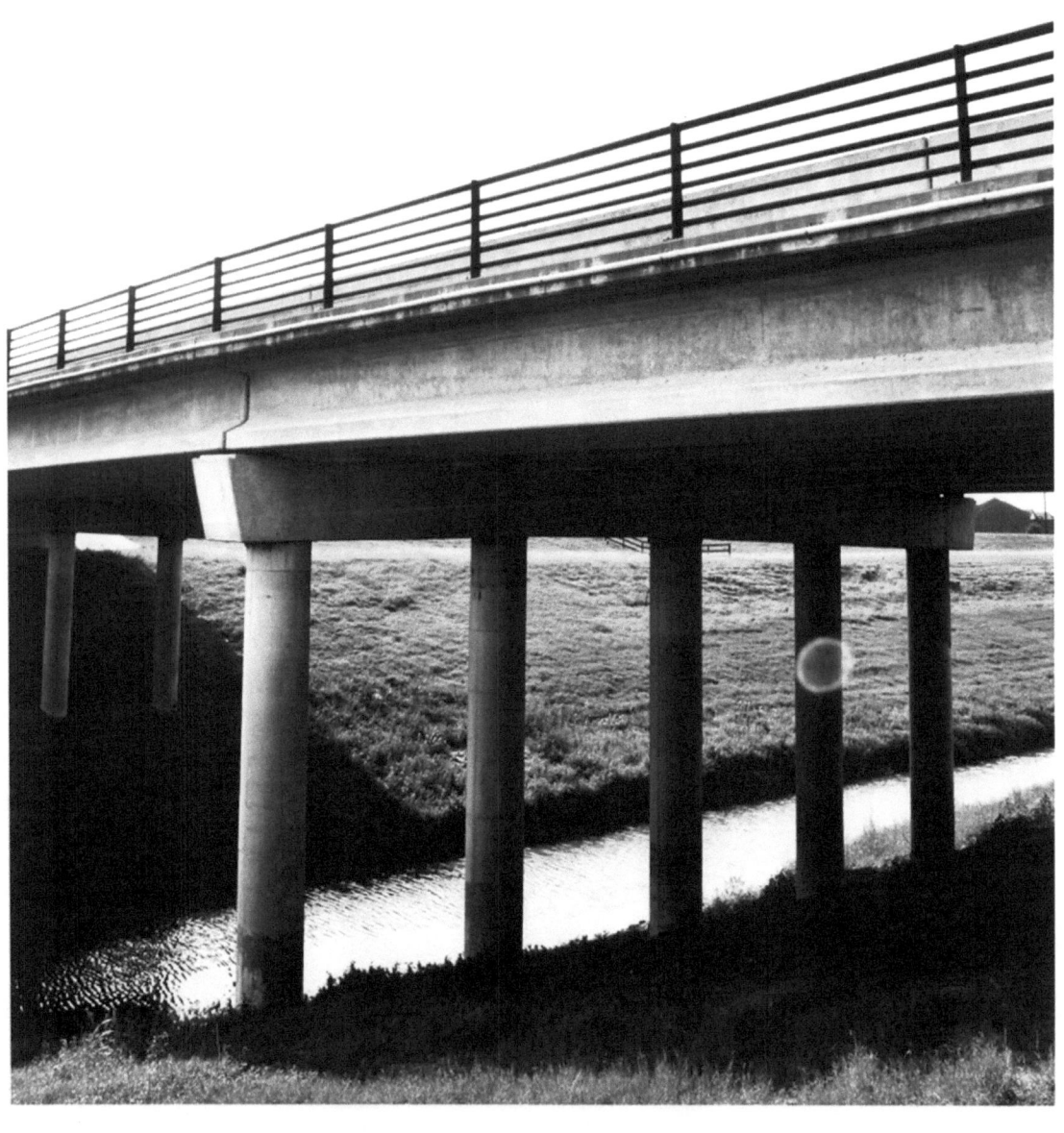

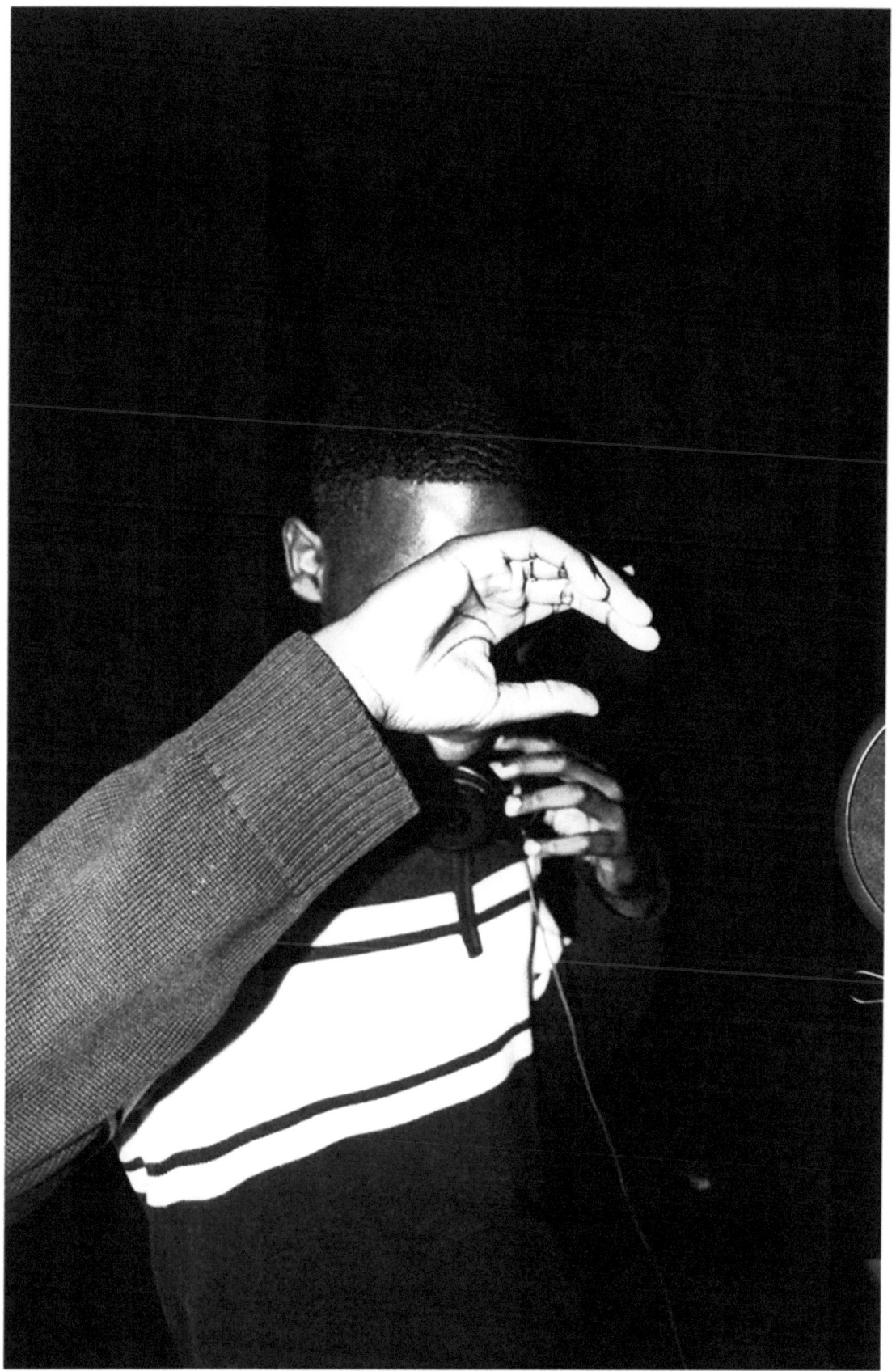

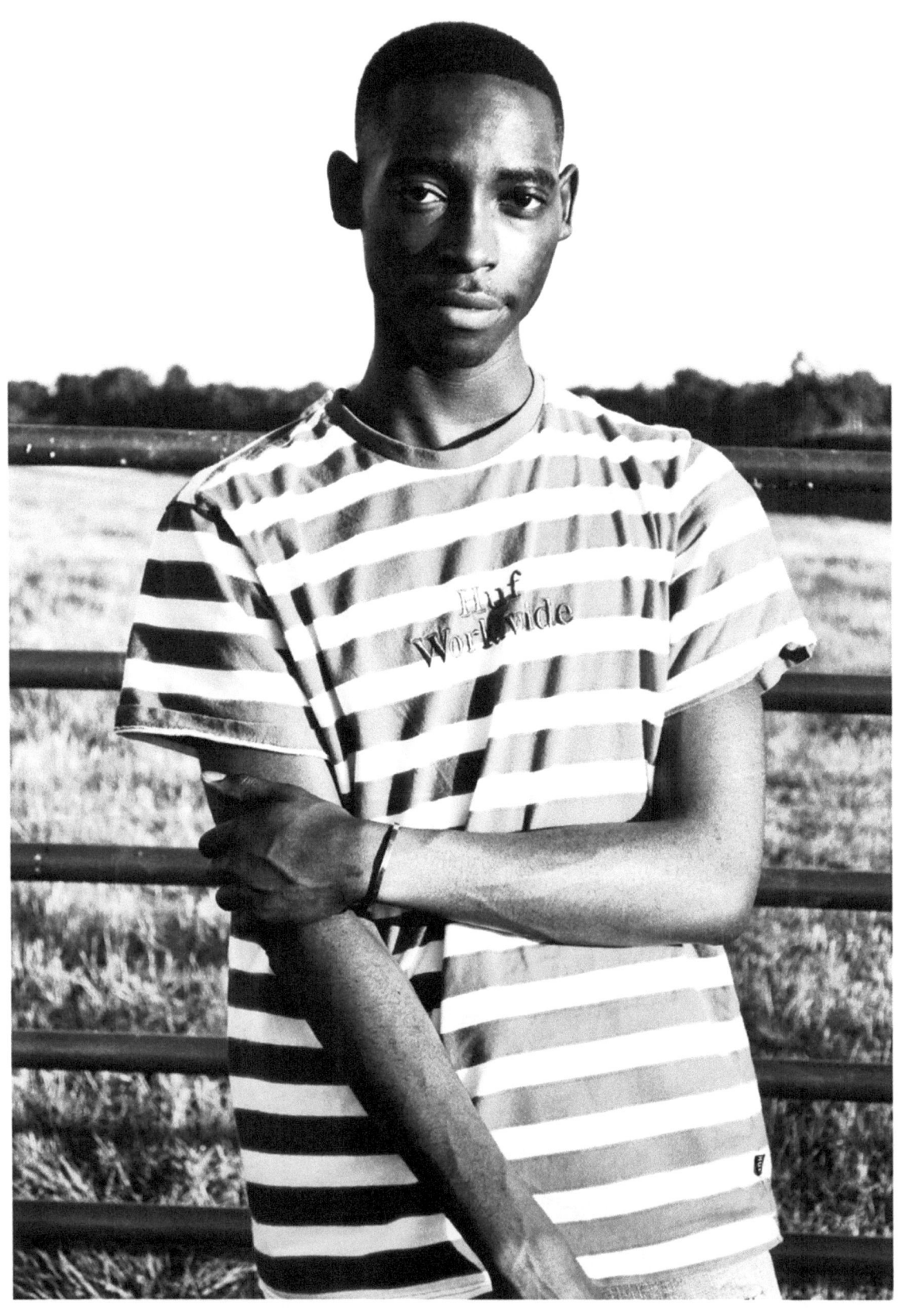

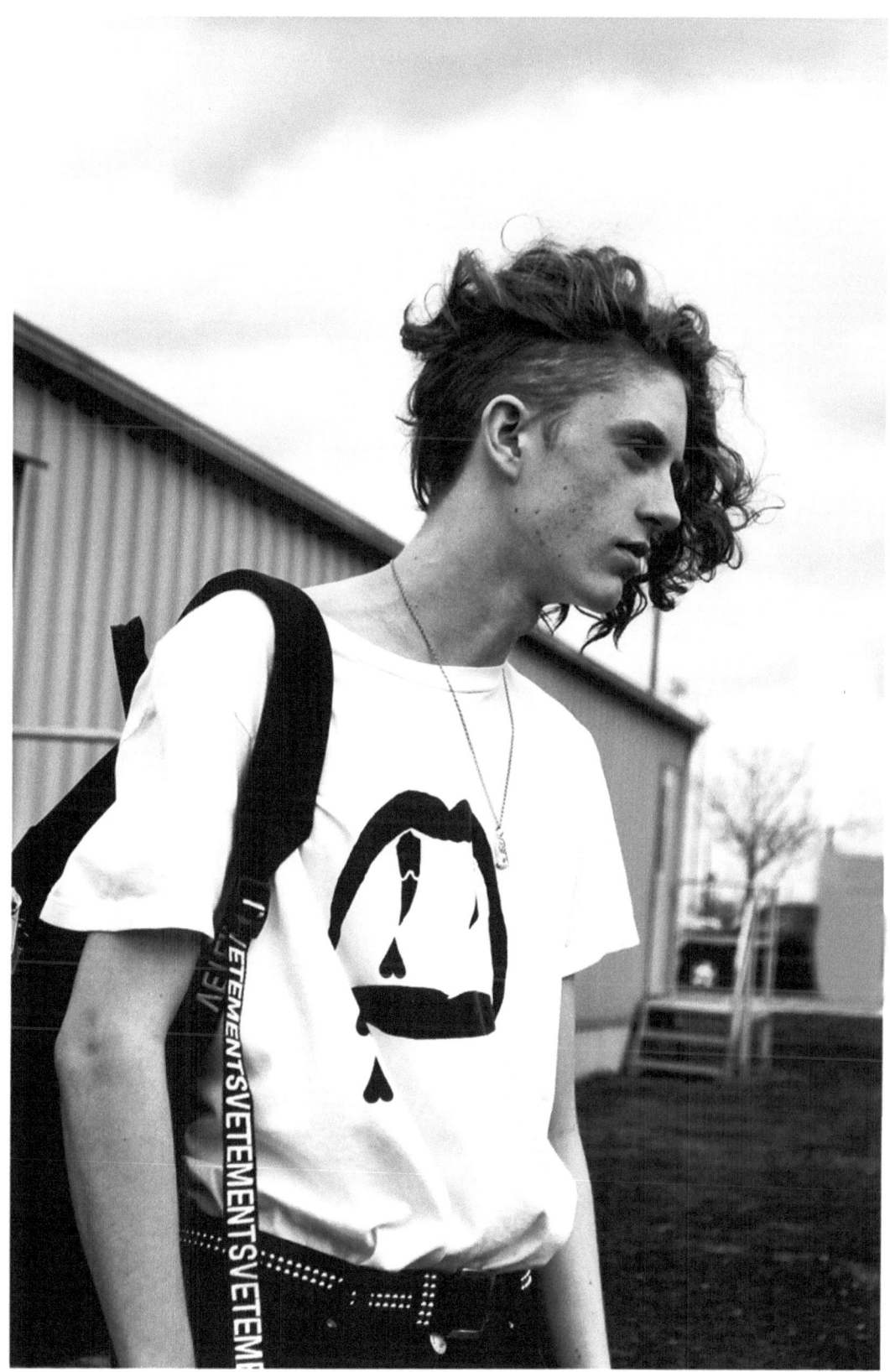

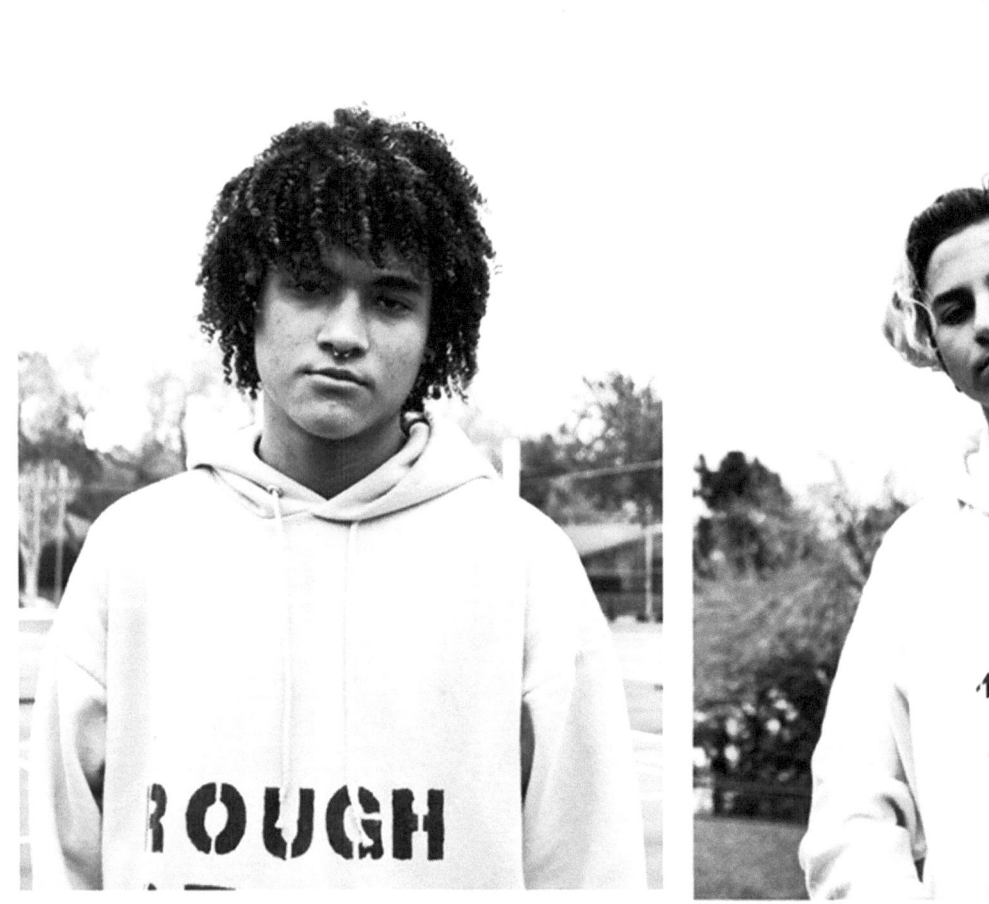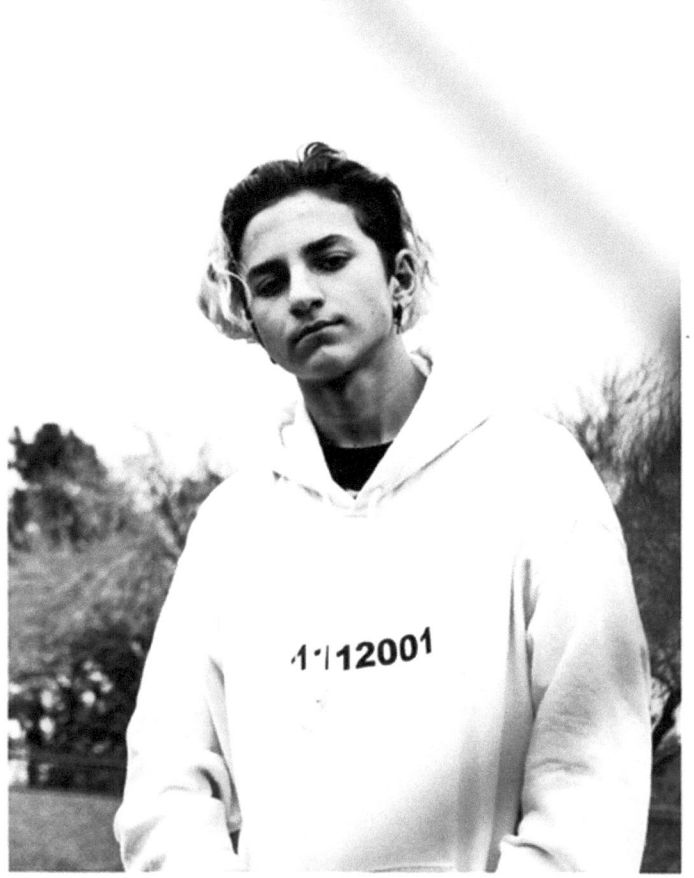

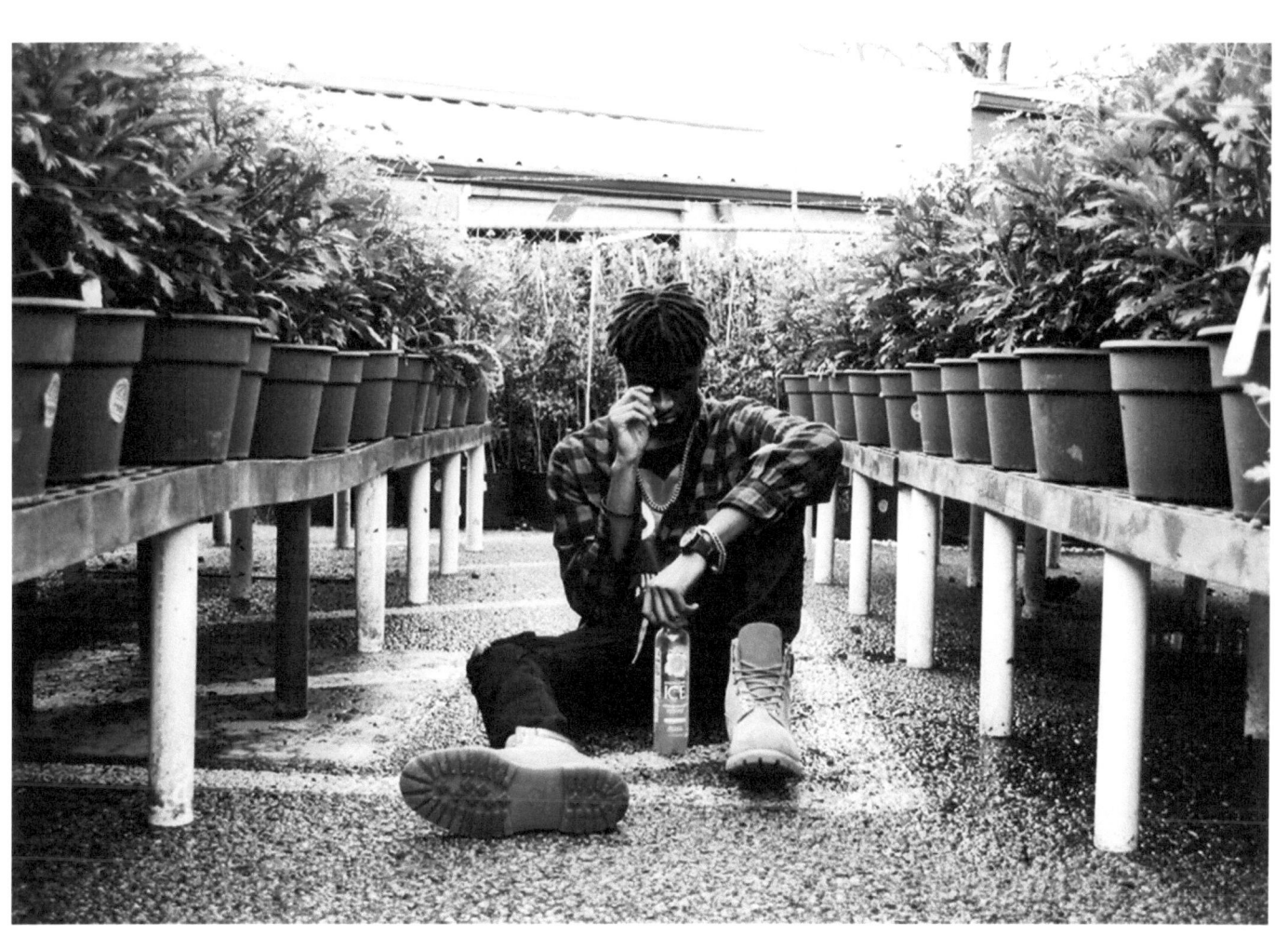

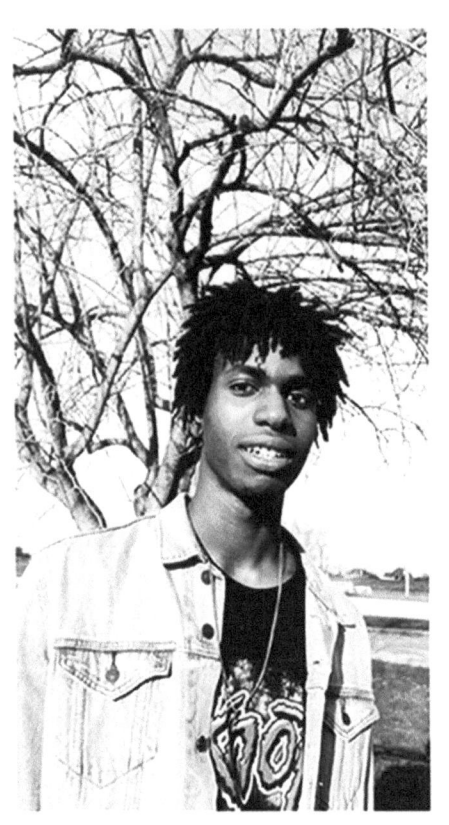 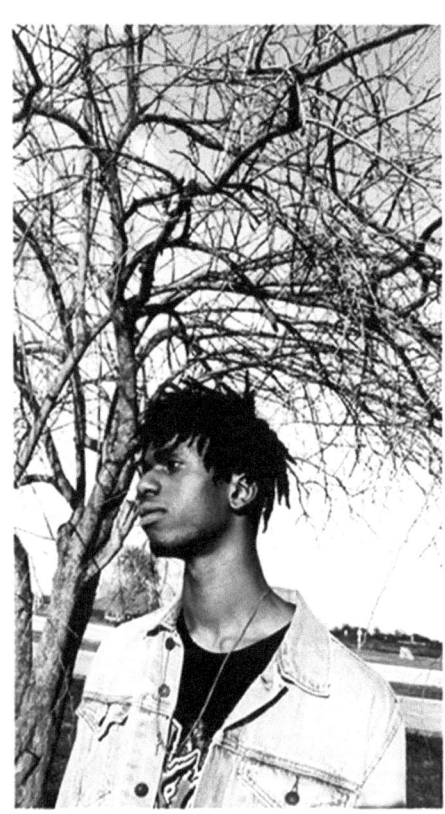 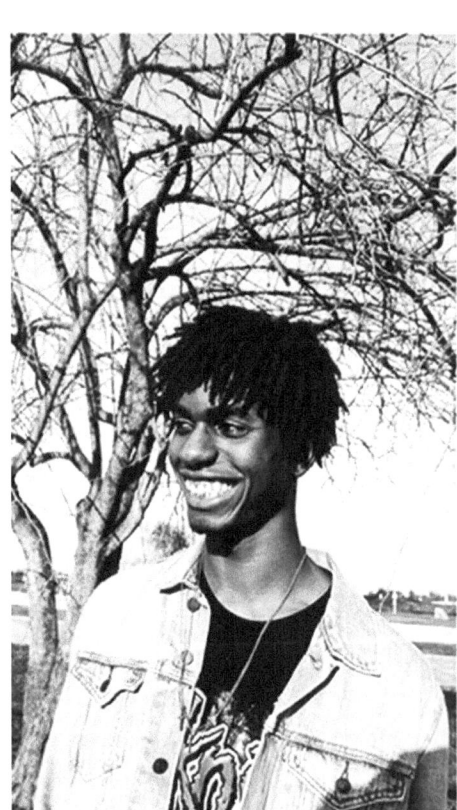

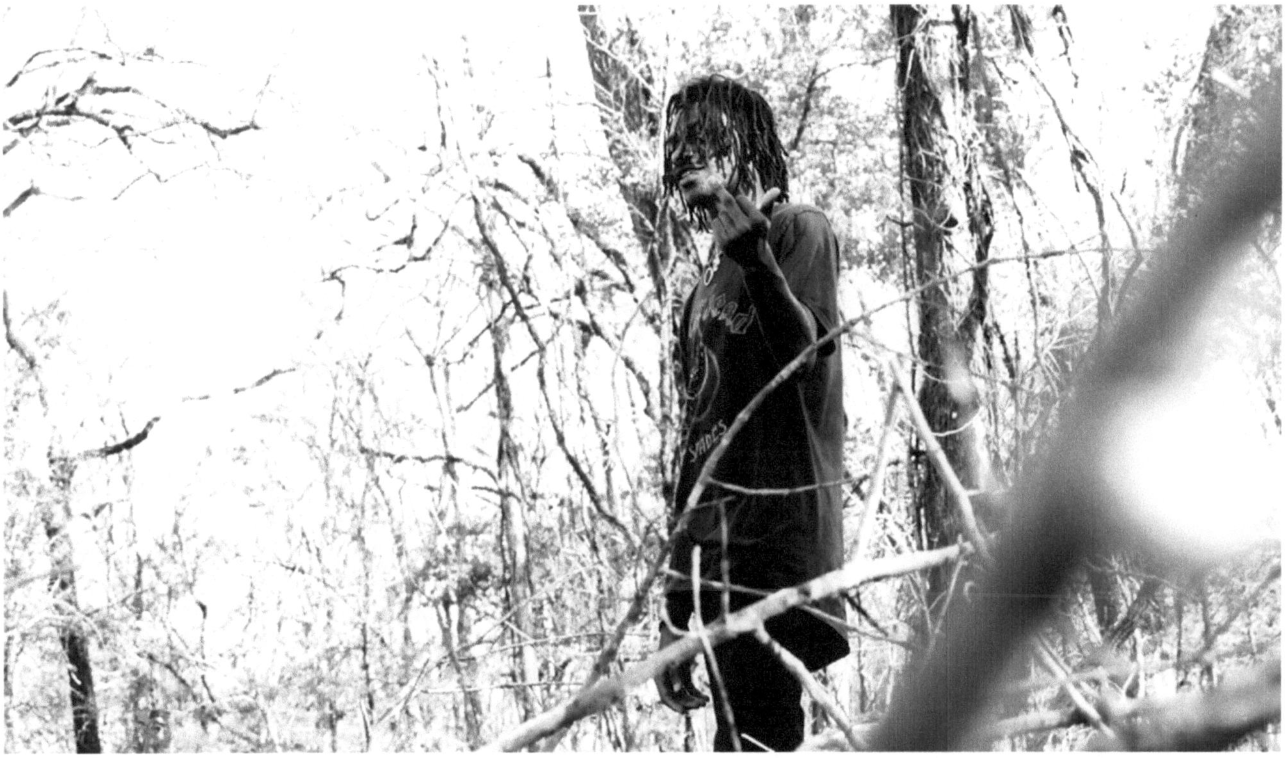

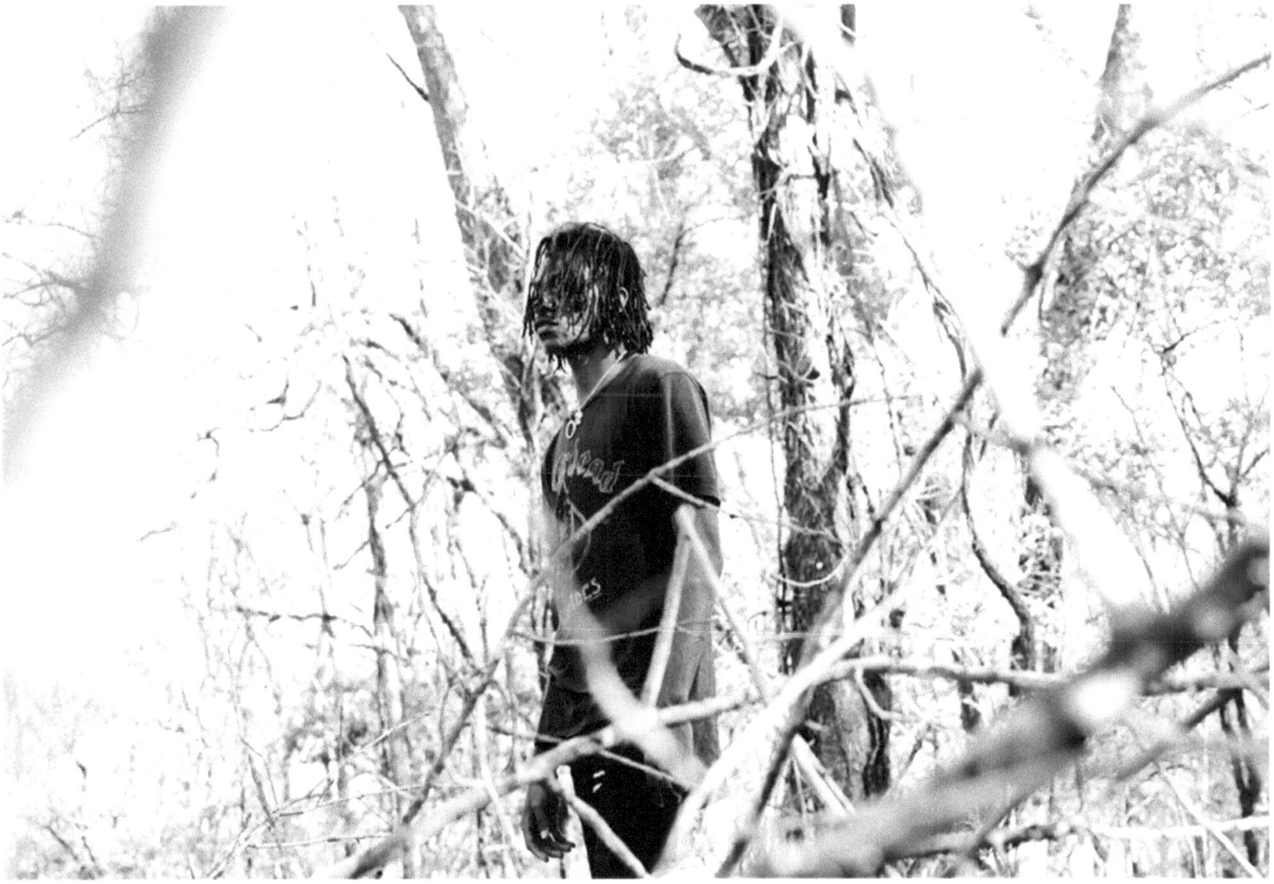

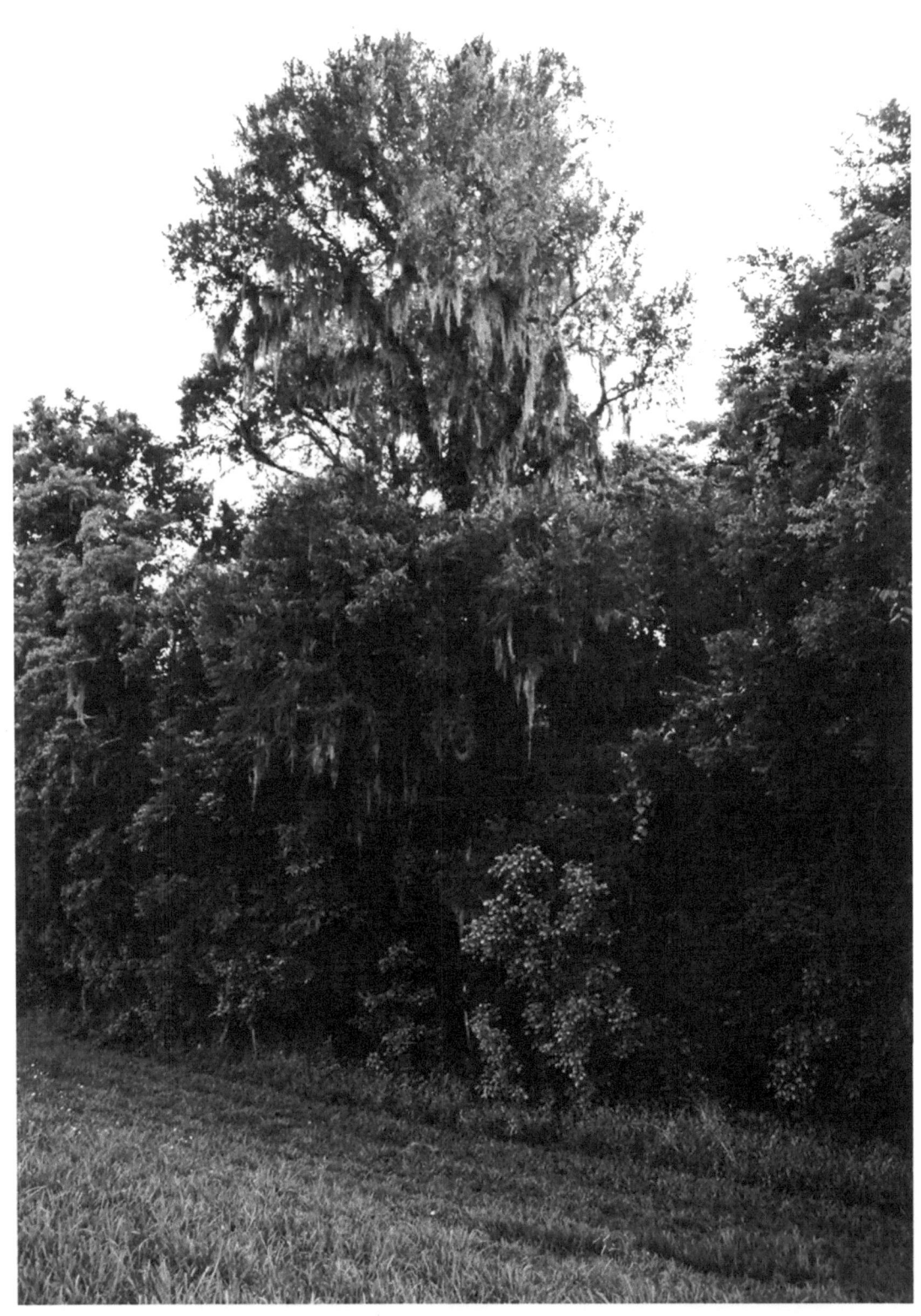

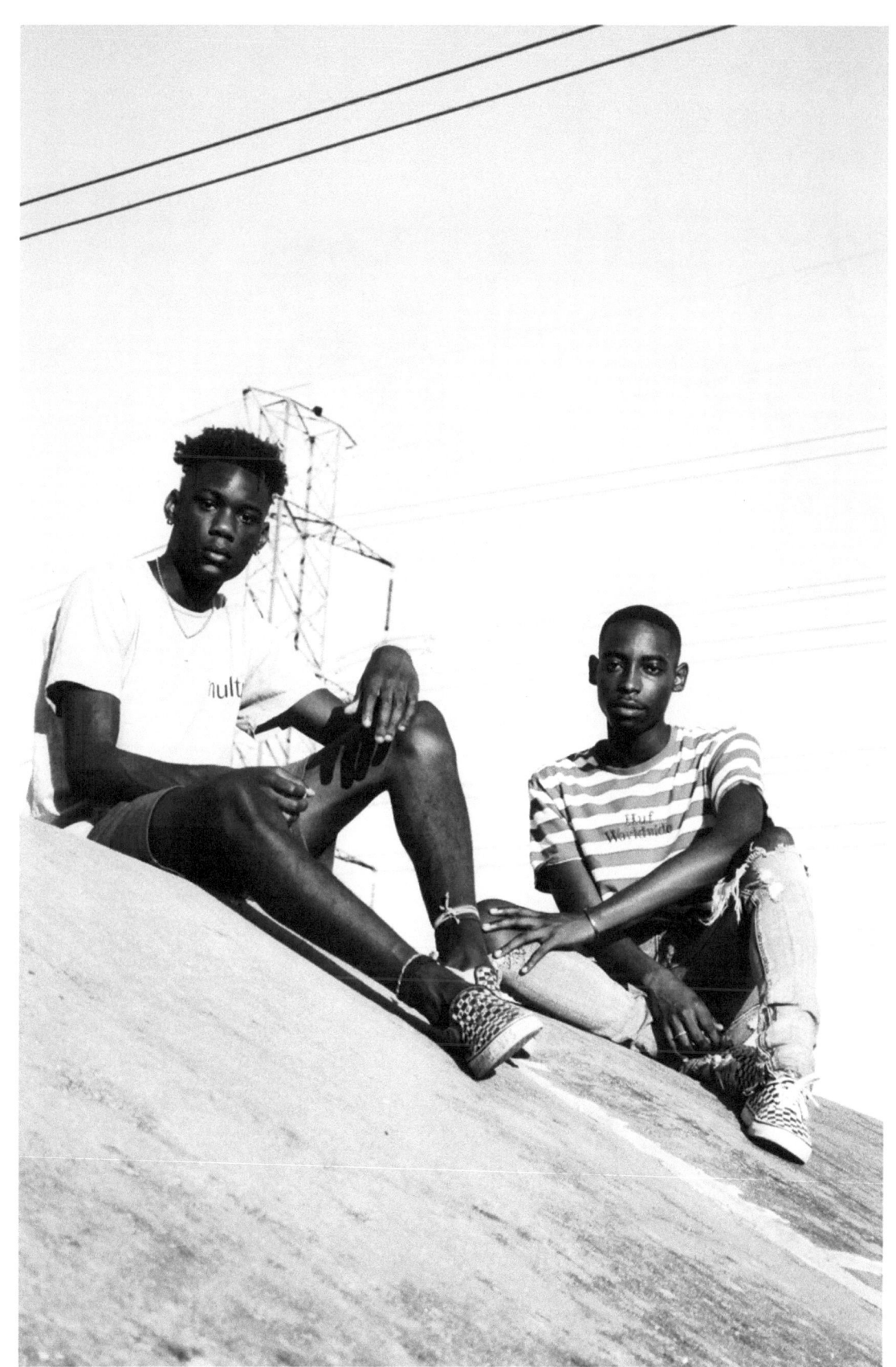

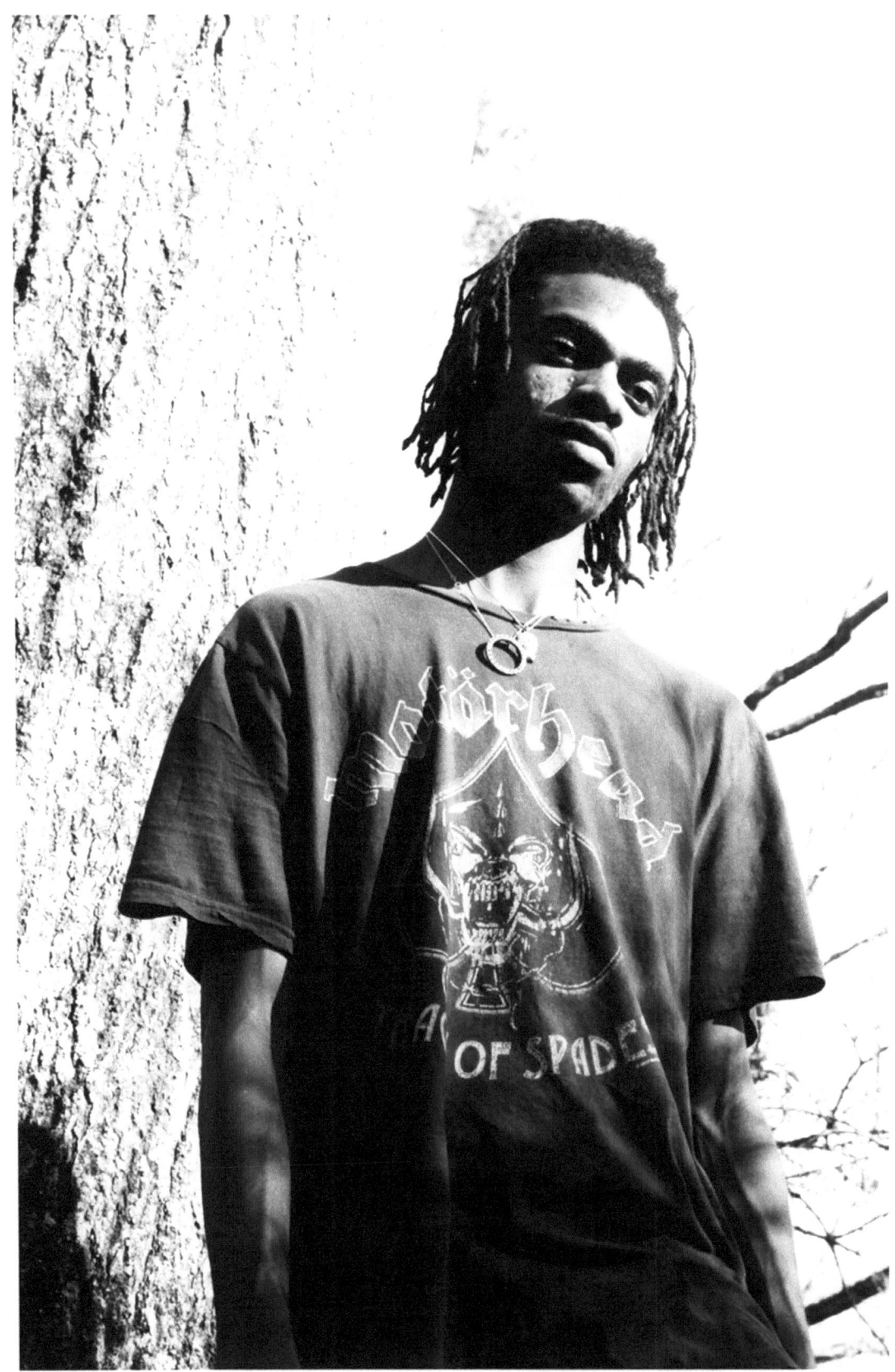

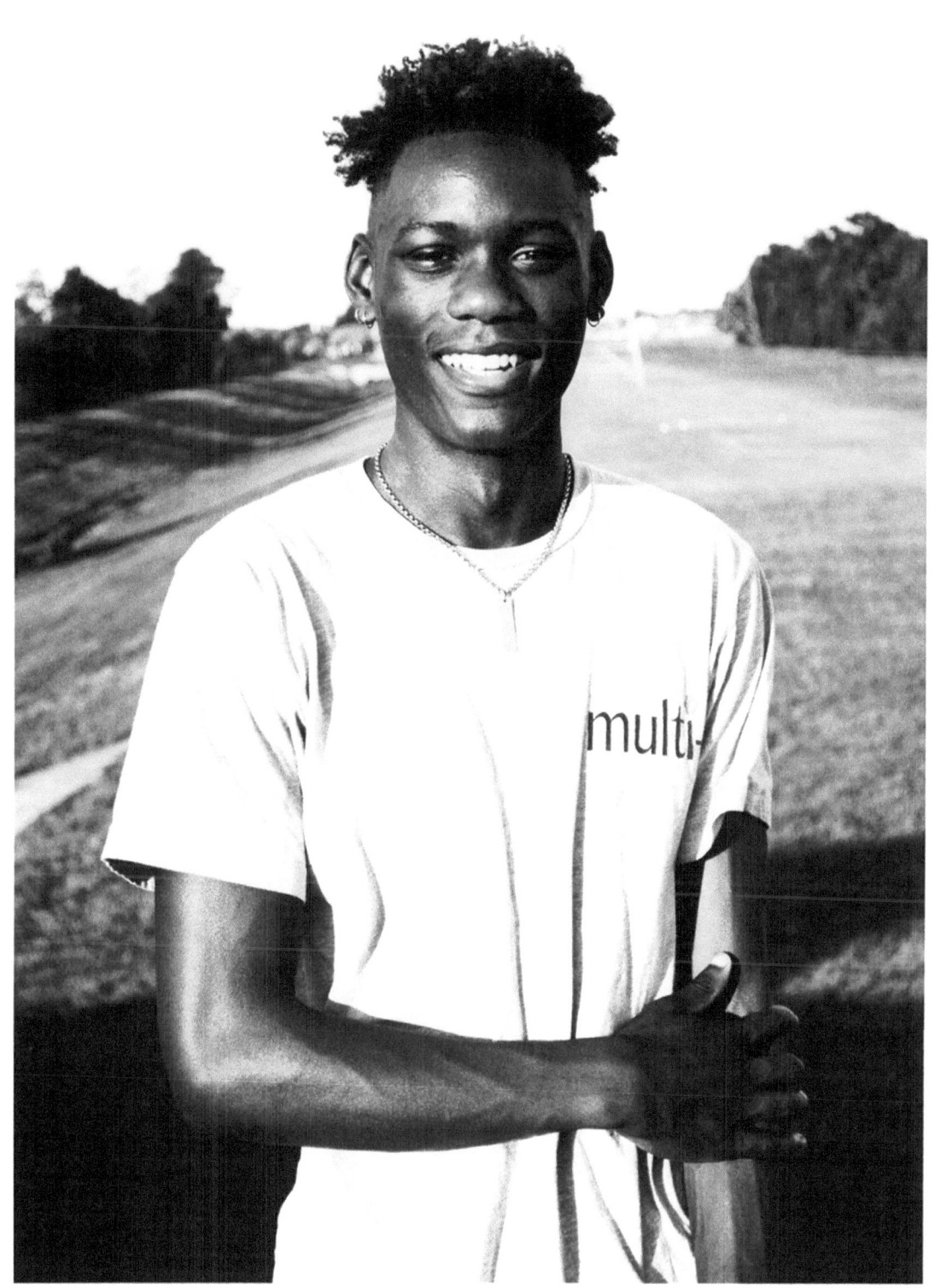

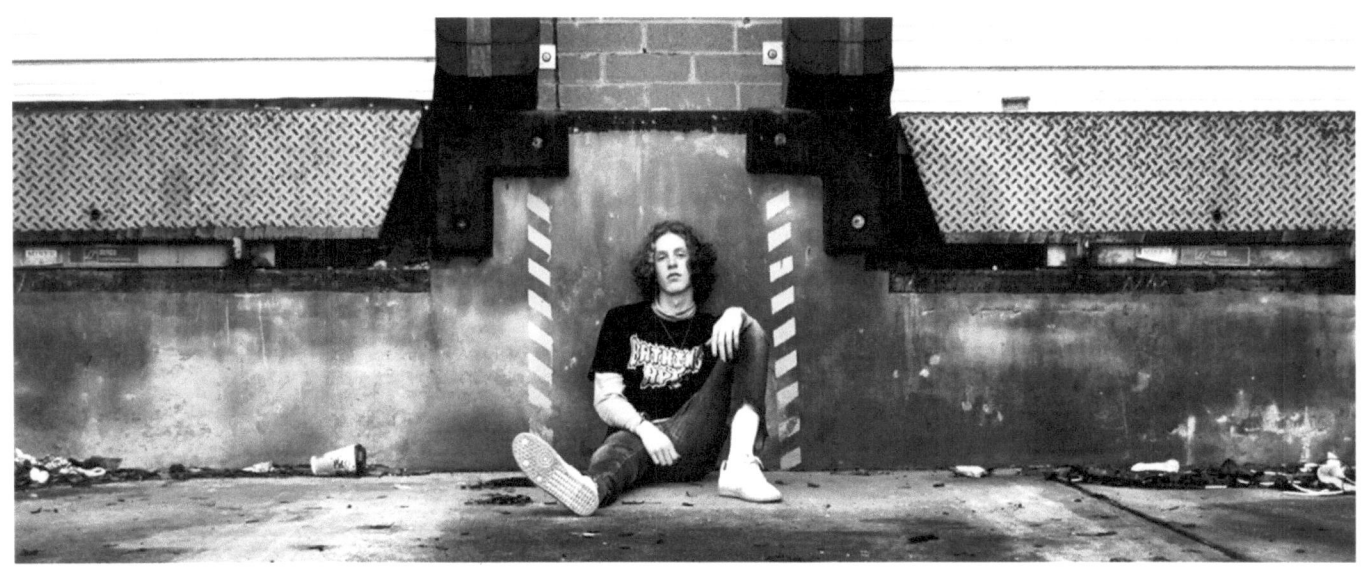

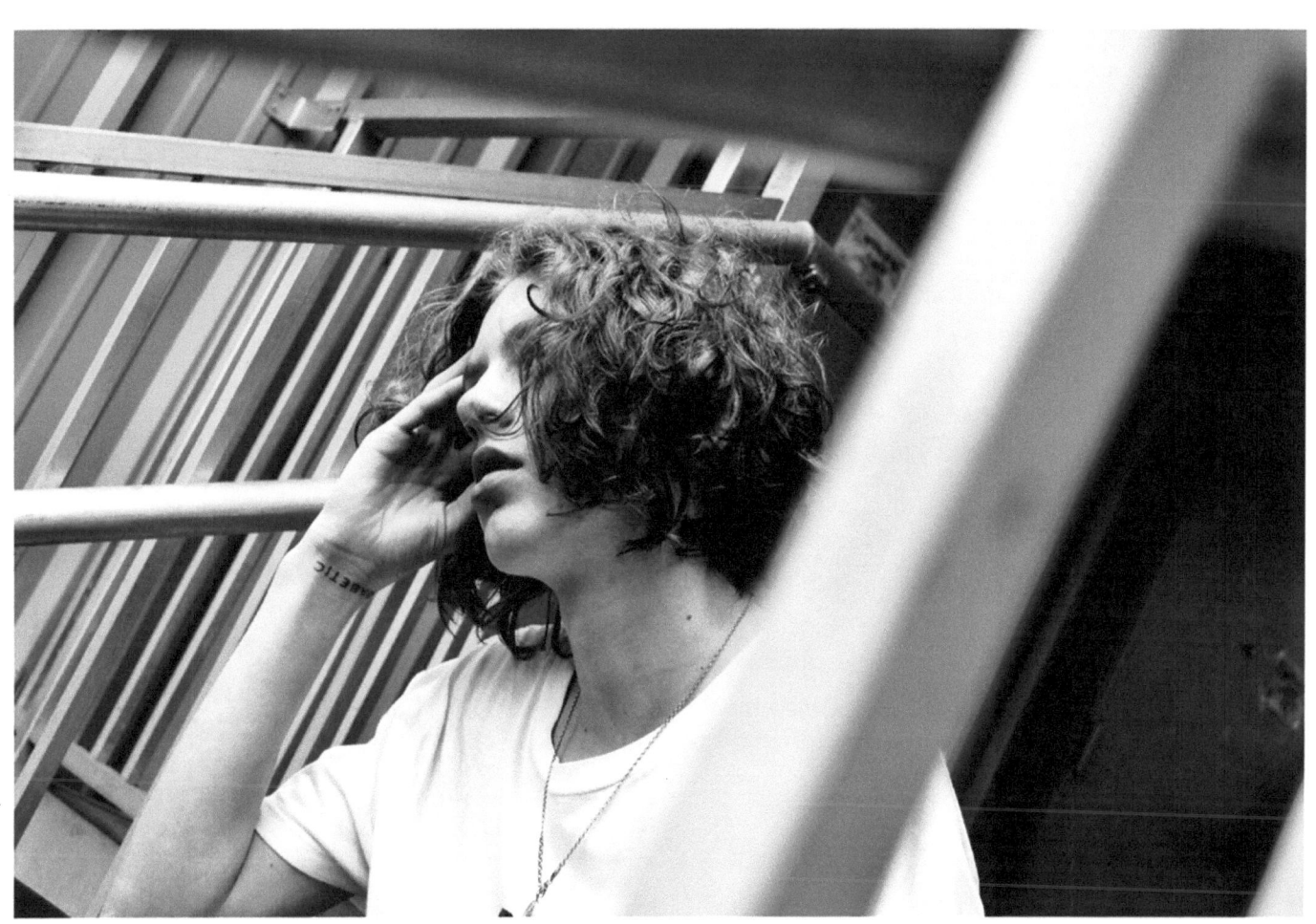

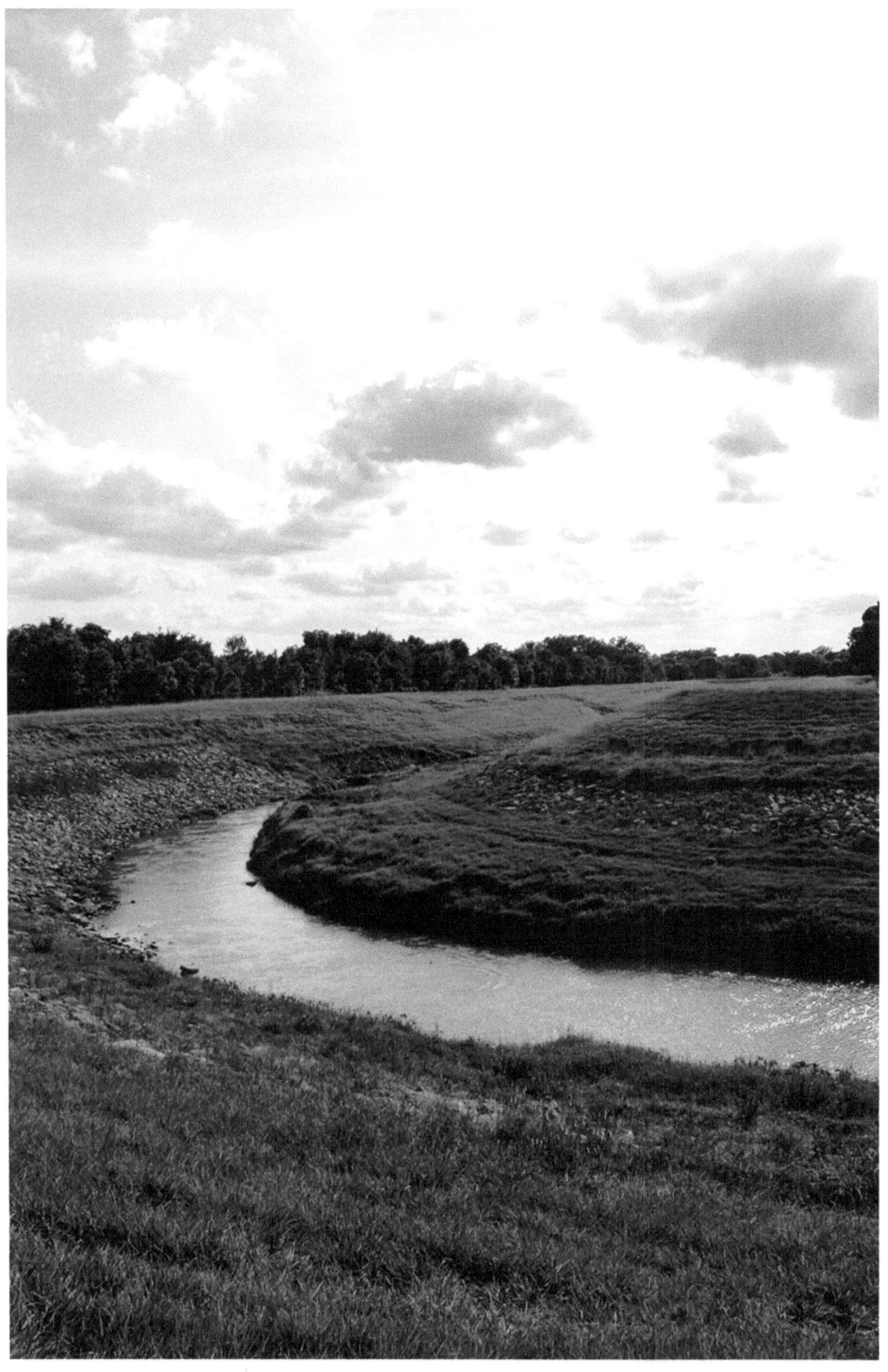

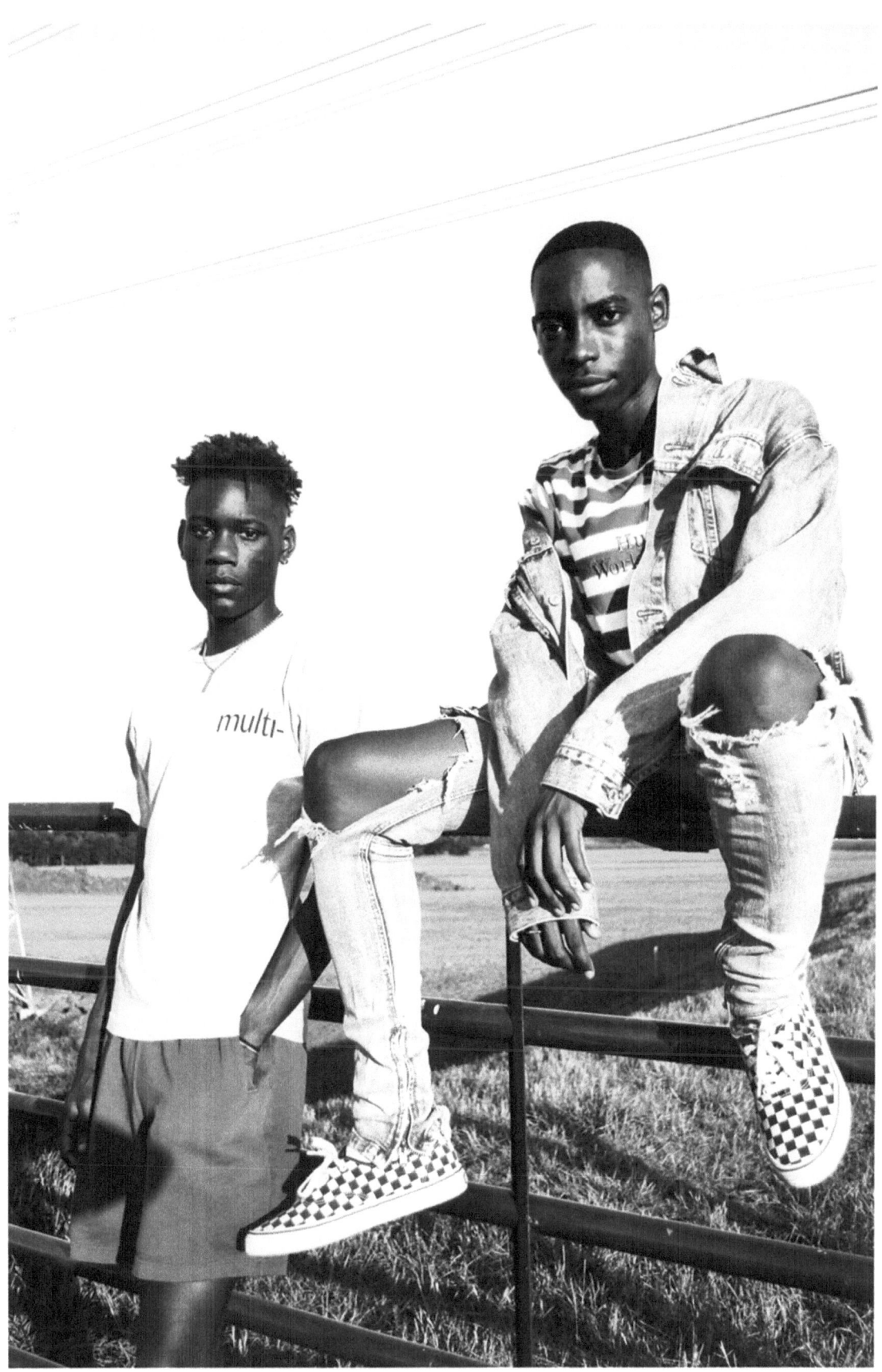

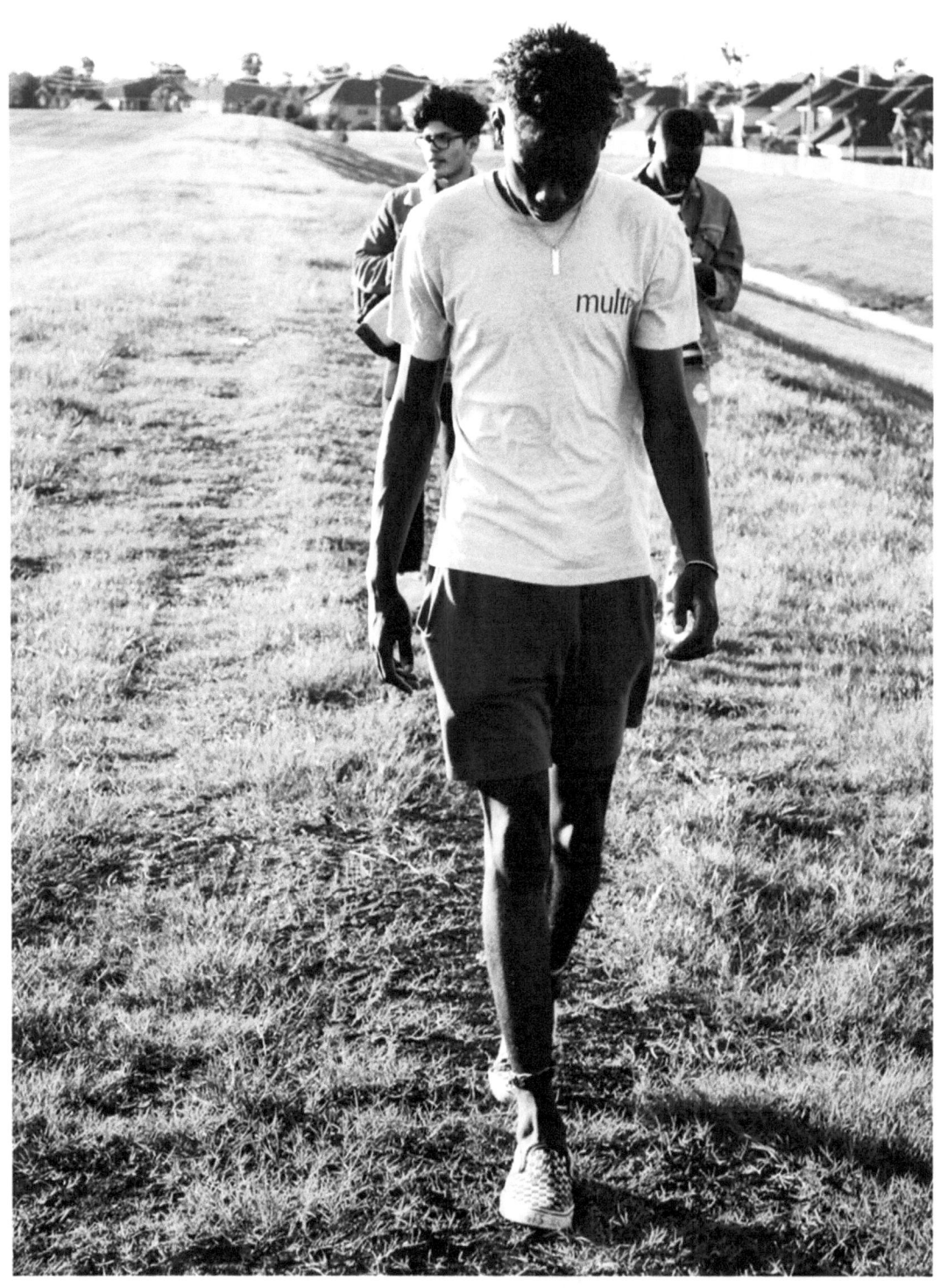

Special Thanks

Courtney Koko

Tyran Jones

Nduka Awa

Jaden Stapler

Trevor Brannan

Tammer Alhaddad

Savion Calvin

Silas Seth Jones

Matheos Michalis

Photography by:
Taj Anthony

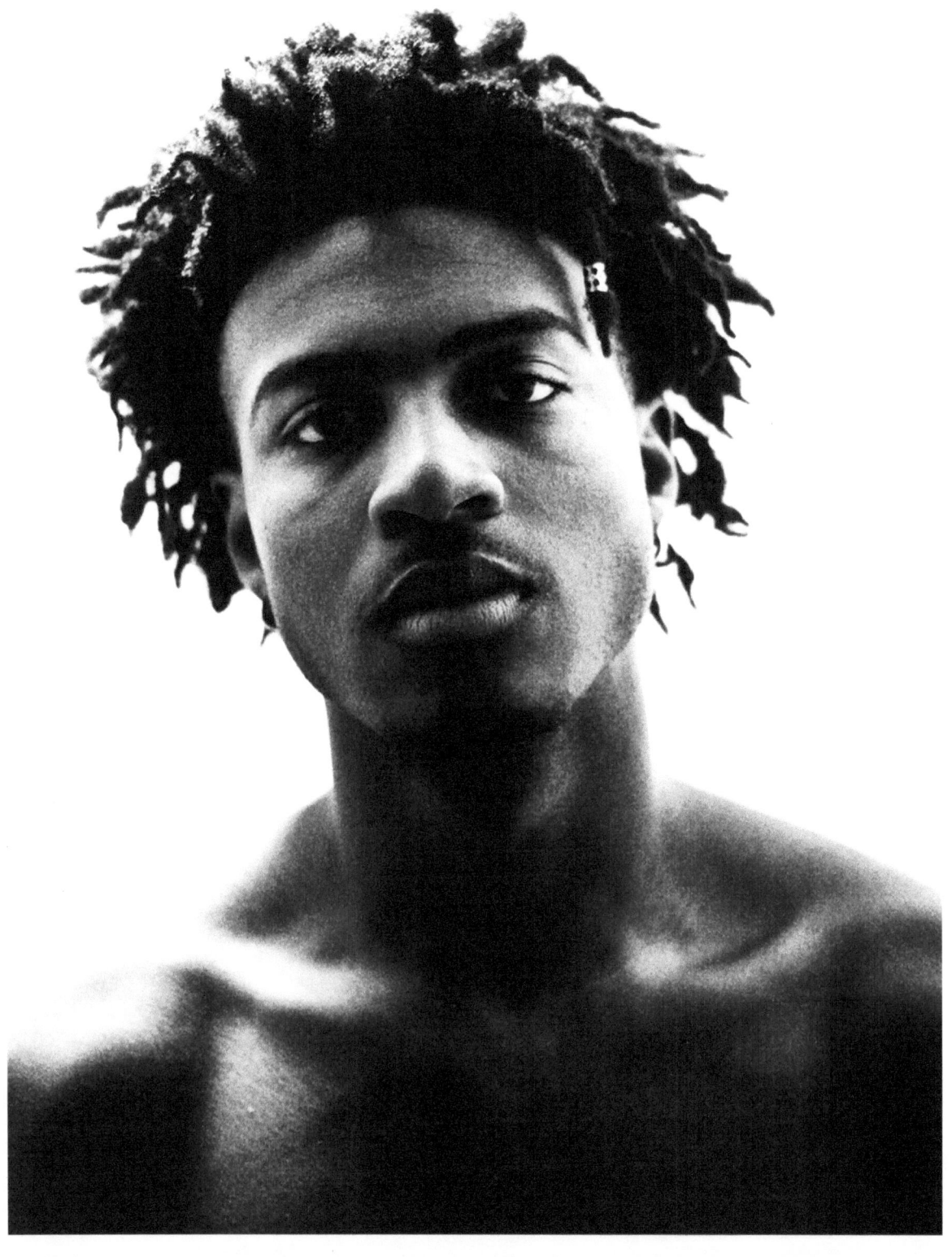

www.ingramcontent.com/pod-product-compliance
Lightning Source LLC
Chambersburg PA
CBHW051825210526
45473CB00005B/1749